TOOLS FOR TEACHERS

- **ATOS:** 0.9
- **LEXILE:** 80L
- **CURRICULUM CONNECTIONS:** patterns, sorting
- **WORD COUNT:** 57

Skills to Teach

- **HIGH-FREQUENCY WORDS:** a, at, has, is, look, the, what
- **CONTENT WORDS:** field, geese, leaves, pattern, pumpkins, shirt, turkey
- **PUNCTUATION:** periods, question marks, exclamation point
- **WORD STUDY:** long /e/, spelled ie (field), ee (geese), ea (leaves), ey (turkey); s, pronounced /s/ (geese), /z/ (leaves, pumpkins); r-controlled vowels (pattern, shirt, turkey)
- **TEXT TYPE:** factual description

Before Reading Activities

- Read the title and give a simple statement of the main idea.
- Have students "walk" though the book and talk about what they see in the pictures.
- Introduce new vocabulary by having students predict the first letter and locate the word in the text.
- Discuss any unfamiliar concepts that are in the text.

After Reading Activities

Write the book's language pattern in two columns on the board: "Look at the ____." and "What is the pattern?" Encourage children to look around the room and identify things that have patterns. Write their answers under the first column. Then identify and discuss the different kinds of patterns they see (stripes, spots, etc.), and write them down under the second column.

Tadpole Books are published by Jump!, 5357 Penn Avenue South, Minneapolis, MN 55419, www.jumplibrary.com

Copyright ©2018 Jump. International copyright reserved in all countries. No part of this book may be reproduced in any form without written permission from the publisher.

Editor: Jenny Fretland VanVoorst **Designer:** Anna Peterson

Photo Credits: Shutterstock: Hawk777, cover; mayakova, 1; MaskaRad, 2–3; TasiPas, 2–3; tonyz20, 2–3; Ana Gram 4–5; B Brown, 6–7; Sensay, 8–9; Irina Rogova, 10–11; kudla, 12–13; Grigorita Ko, 14–15.

Library of Congress Cataloging-in-Publication Data
Names: Mayerling, Tim, author.
Title: Patterns in fall / by Tim Mayerling.
Description: Minneapolis, Minnesota : Jump!, Inc., (2017) | Series: Patterns in the seasons | Audience: Ages 3–6.
Identifiers: LCCN 2017018072 (print) | LCCN 2017021681 (ebook) | ISBN 9781624966033 (ebook) | ISBN 9781620317563 (hardcover: alk. paper) | ISBN 9781620317761 (pbk.)
Subjects: LCSH: Autumn—Juvenile literature. | Pattern perception—Juvenile literature.
Classification: LCC QB637.7 (ebook) | LCC QB637.7 .M39 2017 (print) | DDC 508.2—dc23
LC record available at https://lccn.loc.gov/2017018072

PATTERNS IN FALL

by Tim Mayerling

TABLE OF CONTENTS

Patterns in Fall 2

Words to Know 16

Index 16

tadpole
books

PATTERNS IN FALL

Look at the leaves.

What is the pattern?

Look at the geese.

What is the pattern?

Look at the field.

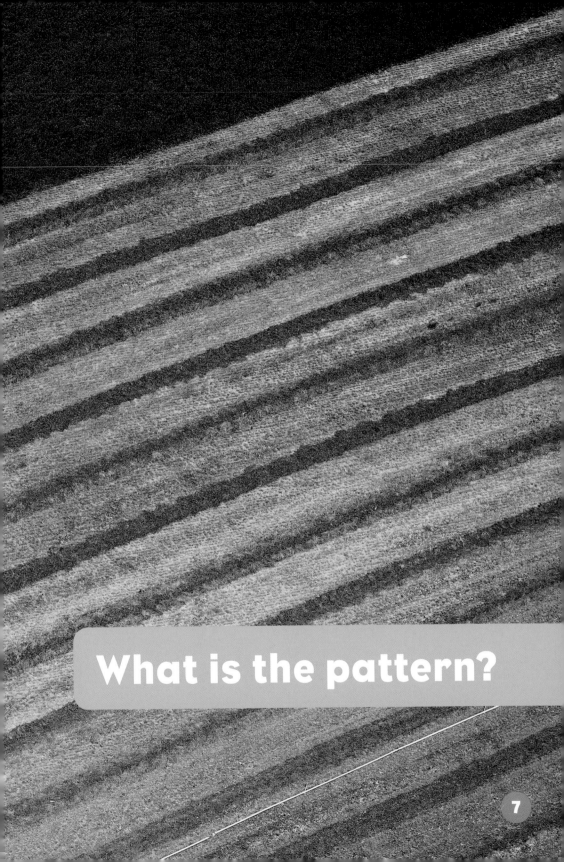

What is the pattern?

turkey

Look at the turkey.

What is the pattern?

Look at the shirt.

What is the pattern?

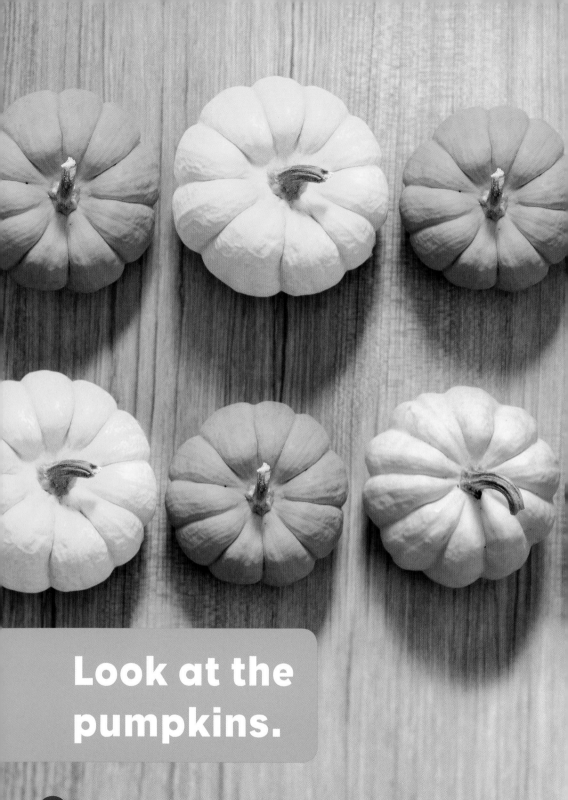

Look at the
pumpkins.

What is the pattern?

Look!

What else has
a pattern?

WORDS TO KNOW

field

geese

leaves

pumpkins

shirt

turkey

INDEX

field 6

geese 4

leaves 2

pattern 3, 5, 7, 9, 11, 13, 15

pumpkins 12

shirt 10

turkey 8